How Bridges Are Made

Text   Jeremy Kingston
Design   Arthur Lockwood

Contents

Facts On File Publications
New York, New York ● Bicester, England

All kinds of bridges

Imagine the world without bridges. The smallest river would become a barrier, only to be crossed by boat, or at a place where the water is shallow enough to wade through. Railways and motorways would be impossible dreams. Journeys that are just a few miles as the crow flies would have to follow a roundabout route to avoid difficult streams and rivers. And if there were heavy loads to be carried, the journey would take even longer. Without bridges, all communication would slow down: and without swift, reliable communications civilization would not be able to develop beyond the stage of small and mainly isolated settlements.

The importance of bridges in early times is shown by the title of one of the chief priests of Ancient Rome – **Pontifex Maximus**, which means chief bridge-builder. This title was later used by the Roman emperors, and then by the Pope, who is still known as the Supreme Pontiff.

There is still something mysterious about a great bridge. The spans look impossibly long, and the supports impossibly slender. But behind the appearance of the most spectacular bridges, as behind that of the most familiar motorway footbridge, lies a store of knowledge going back hundreds of years. This knowledge is increasing all the time, as new materials and new techniques are tested.

The early bridge-builders found, through experience, ways of ensuring that their bridges did not collapse by making them thicker and heavier than was strictly necessary. In the massive stone bridges of Roman days there were no shallow arches. They were almost all semi-circular, and the width of the piers supporting them had to be as much as one third of the span. The greatest span on the magnificent Pont du Gard near Nîmes in the South of France is 100 feet (30.5 metres).

A fallen tree-trunk or single stone slab was the earliest form of beam bridge. The introduction of a pier allowed wider rivers to be spanned, as in this stone 'clapper' bridge at Postbridge on Dartmoor, Devon, England. The date is unknown but the design is certainly prehistoric.

The Pont du Gard near Nîmes, France, constructed in about 19BC to transport water across the River Gard. A superb example of Roman bridge-building, its parapet is 160 feet (49 metres) above the valley floor.

Compare this with the streamlined Gladesville Bridge in Sydney, Australia (shown on page 17), which was opened in 1964. It is still an arch bridge, but instead of stone blocks it has hollow boxes of reinforced concrete. Because of the progress made in the use of materials, the Gladesville Bridge became the first stone (or concrete) arch to span 1000 feet (305 metres).

From wood and stone to steel and concrete, each material is used in its own particular way and has its own advantages and shortcomings. The final appearance of a bridge – its size, style and material – is the result of the designer's answer to a series of important questions. What height must the bridge be above the water? What is the ground like at the banks? Can piers be built in the river? How many spans should there be? How much traffic is expected? How much will it cost?

This book first explains the difference between the basic styles of bridge – beam, arch, suspension and cantilever. Next it tells you why steel and concrete are the materials preferred by engineers today: then how these materials are used in different kinds of bridges.

In the Middle Ages, when the techniques of the Romans had been largely forgotten, it was thought that some bridges could only have been built with the help of the Devil! Understanding how a structure is made may take away some of the mystery, but it does mean that the credit goes where it should – to the skills and ingenuity of the human race.

The Golden Gate Suspension Bridge across the entrance to San Francisco Bay. Completed in 1937, its span of 4200 feet (1280 metres) remained the longest in the world for nearly thirty years.

The main types of bridge

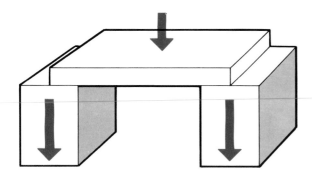

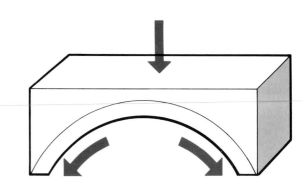

Beam

This can be just a plank of wood, or it may be a complicated structure of girders. The horizontal beam is supported at each end, either by the ground or on piers. The main points of weakness are between the supports, where the weight tends to bend the beam downwards, squeezing the upper surface (compression) and stretching the lower (tension).

Arch

Here the weight is carried outwards along two curving paths. The points where the arch reaches the ground (called the **abutments**) resist the outward thrust and keep the bridge up. The roadway can be carried on top of the arch, or it may cut through the arch so that the two ends support the road from below while the centre supports it from above. This is called a **through arch**.

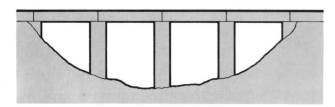

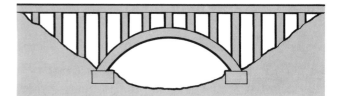

The four long-established types of bridge shown above have recently been joined by a fifth type:

Cable-stayed

The cable-stayed bridge is a newcomer, developed by German engineers and first seen in its pure form in the 600-foot (183-metre) span at Strömsund, Sweden, in 1956. The deck is supported from cables connected directly to towers. At first there were pairs of towers, but in later examples single towers were built in the central reservation of the deck. Though it is still rare, this design – midway between beam and suspension – is likely to become increasingly familiar. It requires fewer piers than the beam bridge, and is more suitable than the suspension bridge for shorter spans.

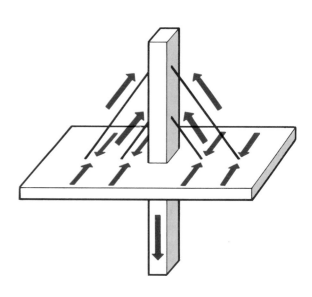

Right: The Luling Bridge spans the Mississippi River at New Orleans. In this example of a two-plane cable-stayed bridge all the cables are connected to the top of the towers.

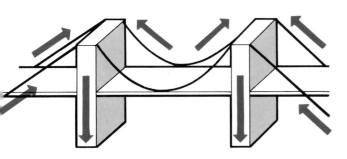

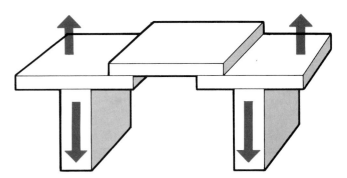

Suspension

The deck, or traffic-way, is suspended by **hangers** (suspenders) from a continuous cable anchored at each end of the bridge. The cables carry the weight up to the top of the towers which transfer it to the ground. The cables of modern bridges are made of thousands of steel wires bound tightly together. As steel stands up well to the effects of tension (stretching), the suspension bridge is the most suitable for long spans.

Cantilever

A beam can be made to support another beam at one end provided that the other end is anchored or weighted down sufficiently. Two planks or beams can be built out towards each other and joined by resting a smaller beam across the free ends. This is how a cantilever bridge works.

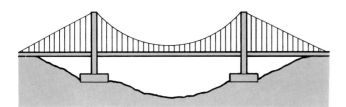

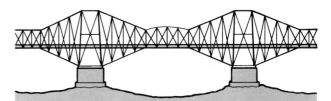

Materials: steel

Steel is iron refined until it is almost free from impurities. Some carbon is left (up to 2½%), and other substances can be added, to produce steels of different strengths and hardness. The problems of manufacture are well understood today, but at one time the production process took so long that steel was used only to make swords and other weapons. Iron was also difficult to produce in large quantities, and was not used as a building material until the 18th century.

The first iron bridge to be built was in 1779 across the River Severn in Coalbrookdale, England. As the name suggests, this was then an industrial area. If a stone bridge had been built instead of an iron one, the scaffolding needed to support it during construction would have blocked the busy river. So semi-circular iron ribs were cast in a nearby foundry and were lifted into position by means of a giant hoist, which stood on the river bank. This construction attracted widespread interest, and many iron bridges soon followed. The place where this first metal bridge was built came to be called Ironbridge.

Two kinds of iron were then available: (a) **cast iron** which was poured into moulds to solidify; (b) **worked** or **wrought iron** which was hammered into the required shape. Cast iron is brittle and unreliable when stretched, so it was reserved for arch bridges where it was mainly in compression, while wrought iron was used for truss and suspension bridges. In the early part of the 19th century many suspension bridges were built in the United States, including the first one which was strong enough to carry wheeled traffic. All of them were suspended from chains whose links were made of wrought iron. French engineers pioneered the use of cables made from wrought iron wires, and in 1834 their cable suspension bridge at Fribourg, Switzerland, held the record for length of span (870 feet, 265 metres).

Iron Bridge at Coalbrookdale, Shropshire, England
The first bridge made entirely of iron is still open to 'wheeled traffic', but only prams and bicycles pushed by hand.

The Great Bridge at St Louis, Missouri, designed by James B. Eads and opened in 1874. This was the first steel bridge and the picture shows sections of arch being cantilevered out from the piers to meet in mid-span.

Truss or lattice bridges are relatively simple to construct. Early examples were made of wood but in the United States they were gradually replaced by iron. The 'Howe' truss was built of timber strengthened with vertical iron rods.

The 'Pratt' truss used the opposite arrangement of wooden verticals and iron diagonals.

Squire Whipple introduced an all-iron truss and went on to design this bowstring truss. Thousands of railway bridges were erected to these designs.

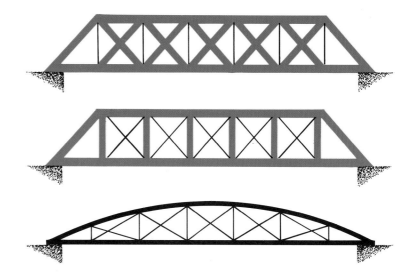

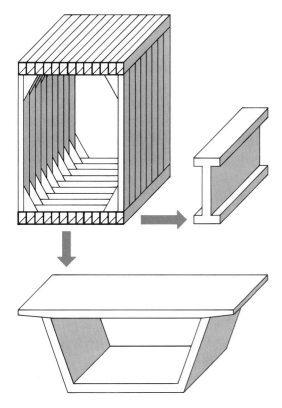

The rectangular tube designed by Stephenson for the Britannia Bridge, Menai Straits, gave rise to the I-girder, sometimes called a plate-girder. It also inspired the modern box-girder, which is aerodynamically shaped to resist wind-pressure and the effects of twist.

The first suspension bridges were not able to cope with the demands of the railways, as the rhythmic loads (that is, the constant movement of vehicles, etc) set up powerful vibrations which literally shook them to their foundations. Several bridges were destroyed in this way – in the United States one was actually brought down by a flock of sheep!

When a railway bridge was needed across the Menai Straits, which separate the mainland of Wales from the island of Anglesey, the first structure which was suggested – a two-arch bridge – was rejected because it would have interfered with shipping. Robert Stephenson, engineer in charge of the project, arrived at a brilliant solution. Knowing that certain natural objects, such as reeds, are hollow and therefore light, but also strong, he built two gigantic hollow tubes and laid the railway track inside them. The bridge is known, therefore, as the Britannia Tubular Bridge. (Picture page 11.) The safest shape was found to be a rectangular tube, or **box-girder** with its height greater than its width and its sides stiffened to prevent buckling.

In later bridges extensive use was made of built-up prefabricated girders having a single central wall, so that in cross-section it looks like a capital I. With various modifications, this **I-girder** sometimes called a **plate-girder** was used right through the 19th century and on into modern times.

In the 1870s, improved production methods led to a dramatic fall in the price of steel, which soon entirely replaced ordinary iron for every kind of bridge. It was the greater strength of steel that made cantilever bridges possible. In its turn, the cantilever system is used for building other kinds of bridges, carrying heavy material out to the unsupported ends.

In the 1950s a different shape of box-girder was introduced – wider, flatter, and better able to resist wind and other pressures. Even longer spans thus became possible. Two hundred and two years after the construction of the Iron Bridge, its steel descendant was opened across the River Humber.

Materials: concrete

The 19th century was the Age of the Train, the 20th century is the Age of the Road. Since the Second World War, thousands of motorways have been built throughout the world, needing on average one bridge for every mile. The bridges range from large-scale interchanges to the delicate-looking footbridges which are some of the most graceful structures of our time. In towns, massive fly-overs carry the principal routes right over the network of lesser roads. The material that has contributed most to all this tremendous building is **concrete**.

Concrete is composed of sand, stones and cement mixed with water and allowed to dry. As it dries it hardens, but before doing so it can be poured into moulds of almost any shape. While hardening, the concrete shrinks slightly, and the hardening process continues long after it is firm to the touch. If the concrete is made to bear a heavy load at this stage it may alter shape. This alteration is called **creep**. Concrete is inherently strong in **compression** but weak in **tension**, and to overcome this weakness it is reinforced with rods or wires of steel.

The first objects made with **reinforced concrete** were garden flower pots. Fifty years passed before engineers felt sufficiently confident of its strength to use it for bridges. Even then, and for a long time afterwards, many concrete bridges were designed to make people think that they were stone. The arches were roughened to look like stone blocks, or the bridge was faced with stone slabs.

An American lawyer, Thaddeus Hyatt, experimented with concrete beams and recommended that the best way to increase their strength was to place the reinforcement near the bottom of the beam. He also suggested bending the small rods up at places where the beam rested on supports. The French engineer François Hennebique

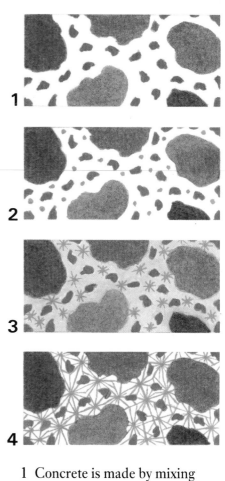

1 Concrete is made by mixing small stones or gravel with sand.
2 Cement powder is next added.
3 Water is poured into the mixture and the cement starts forming into crystals.
4 The crystals grow until they bind the sand and stones together into a solid mass.

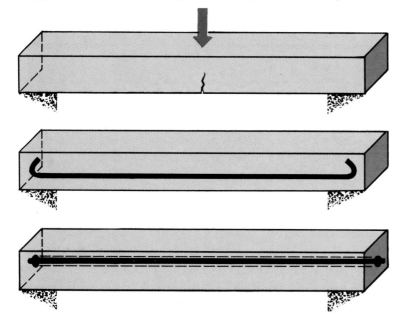

The greatest stress in a concrete beam will occur at the unsupported centre.

Thaddeus Hyatt (d. 1901) recommended this design as the best reinforcement for concrete beams.

Eugène Freyssinet (d. 1962) developed ways for pre-stressing concrete. Wires or rods placed within the concrete can be stretched while the concrete is hardening. Or, tubes can be left in the concrete and wires inserted afterwards, stretched and sealed with cement.

(1842–1921) was the first to use steel reinforcement in place of iron, and his bridge at Liège, Belgium, was regarded as very daring in 1905. Although it has a span of 180 feet (55 metres) the arch at mid-span is only one foot (0.3 metre) deep.

Shapes like this, apparently defying the laws of gravity, are only made possible by the steel reinforcement working within the concrete. Robert Maillart (1872–1940), a Swiss engineer of revolutionary brilliance, understood so perfectly how the stresses worked in his bridges that he was able to use the absolute minimum of material. His designs were chosen because they were economical, but he was seldom entrusted with anything but remote, minor roads. (Picture page 17.) He suffered from being a genius ahead of his time.

Another brilliant French engineer, Eugène Freyssinet (1879–1962), revolutionized methods of reinforcement, with **pre-stressed concrete**. Instead of pouring concrete around a skeleton of metal rods and leaving it to harden, he invented ways of tightening the rods (now more often wires or cables) while the hardening was taking place. When the ends of the rod are released, the solid concrete keeps the rod stretched. If the position of the rods is carefully calculated they will be better able to resist the stresses in the completed bridge.

Pre-stressed concrete is cheaper and easier to use, and many kinds of motorway bridges are made from it. These bridges are purposely varied in shape and appearance to add interest to motorway travel.

Building the Orwell Bridge at Ipswich, Suffolk, England. A temporary peninsula has been built halfway across the river. The picture shows foundations being dug, with steel reinforcement in position and completed piers on the far side.

Structural problems in bridges
1 Bending. Compression occurs in the upper part and tension in the lower.
2 Shear. Parts of the deck gradually slide past each other until breaking point is reached.
3 Buckling of the piers due to compression.
4 In suspension bridges, tension (stretching) occurs in the cables and hangers.
5 Torsion (twist) occurs whenever the weight of the traffic on each side of the deck is unequal.

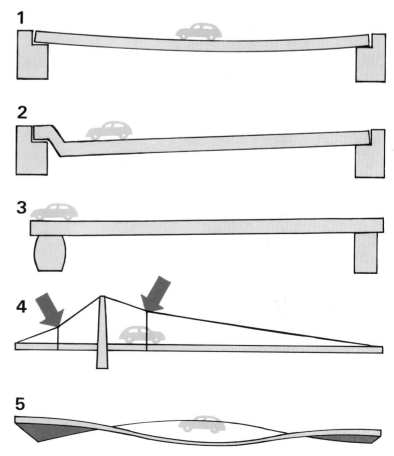

9

▛▜▛ Steel beams and boxes

So that he can work out what stresses a new bridge will have to bear, the engineer has to consider the bridge's own weight, the weight of the traffic that it will carry, and the damaging effect of wind. Wind pressure has destroyed many bridges, and a long deck with solid, vertical walls is particularly at risk. For the decks of today's bridges, therefore, engineers have produced an aerodynamic shape called a **trapezoid** – a hollow box of which, in practice, the upper surface is wider than the lower.

The deck of a large modern steel beam bridge will be made up of a series of separate box units welded together so that they become a continuous box-girder. The picture below shows a unit about to be lowered into position. The smaller drawings explain the different stages of construction. At the Cleddau Bridge in Wales (1975) this method was used to construct all spans except the longest. After an accident in which four men were killed, the last seven units were welded together on shore, floated out to the bridge, and lifted into position. The span weighed 1000 tonnes.

The first ever box beam bridge was the Britannia Tubular Bridge, opened in 1850 (see page 6). It carried the railway line from London to Holyhead across the Menai Straits and was named after the Britannia Rock in

Launching girder with box unit on V-frame ready to be lowered. (See drawing 5).

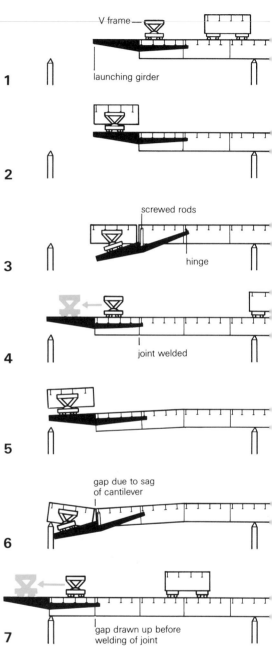

Erection sequence
1 Box to be erected being winched along bridge on bogies.
2 Box transferred to 'V' frame and run to end of launching girder.
3 Launching girder lowered on rods.
4 Launching girder moved forward, next box winched along bridge.
5 Box transferred to 'V' frame and run to end of launching girder.
6 Box landed on pier.
7 Span completed.

Cleddau Bridge, Milford Haven, Wales.
The pre-assembled deck girder has been manoeuvred into position and the lifting cables attached. Lifting the girder 122 feet (37 metres) took 16 hours.

The four tubes of the Britannia Bridge, each weighing over 1,500 tons, were floated out to the foot of the piers on barges and raised 103 feet (31 metres) into position, using hydraulic lifting tackle. Raising the tube shown here took 17 days.

the centre of the Strait, which provided a secure foundation for the central pier. With continuous girder bridges there is a risk of one pier settling and imposing strain on the others, so this type of bridge is not built except where the foundations can be carried down to bedrock, or arrangements made for any settlement.

Before the Britannia Bridge was built, detailed structural tests were carried out. The designer, Robert Stephenson, consulted two specialist engineers who tested materials, experimented with different shapes of tube, and built a 75-foot (23-metre) model. The original design included suspension chains – openings intended to take these can be seen at the top of the towers – but the tests showed that the tubes could be made strong enough to support their own weight and that of the heaviest trains without the need of chains.

⊤⊤⊤ Concrete beams

Along a motorway you will see concrete beam bridges of all shapes and sizes. Most of them cross the road at right angles. Others slant across (these are called 'skew' bridges) or follow a curve. Sometimes one end of an overbridge is higher than the other, and the beam is supported by a sloping pier at the higher end only, giving a rather lop-sided appearance. Bridges may cross the motorway in one span or two. The piers may be all-steel, or steel columns filled with concrete, or reinforced concrete slabs.

Sometimes the motorway itself will become a long bridge, or viaduct, stretching on two parallel rows of piers across a valley or above a junction of lesser roads. Where there is not much space, instead of a double row a single row may be built, with the deck cantilevered out sideways. The design must always suit the needs of each particular situation. The positioning of the piers may depend on certain features which cannot be altered, such as faults in the ground. These will affect the structure and final shape of the bridge.

The special advantage of concrete is that it is a versatile material and unlike steel does not require so much maintenance, which is very costly. The basic costs of constructing a concrete bridge and a steel bridge may be about the same, but the further expense of maintenance could decide the choice in favour of concrete. This is particularly true in built-up areas, where maintenance can be difficult or dangerous, and where there is high industrial pollution.

A large pre-cast beam being placed into position on a road bridge near Gloucester, England.

General view of Maracaibo construction site
1 Automatic concrete mixing plant.
2 Manufacture and storage of pile sections.
3 Joining of pile sections and shipment of piles.
4 Gantry.
5 Manufacture of shuttering (large moulds) for the pier caps. The concrete will be poured at the bridge.
6 Placing reinforcement, pouring concrete and stressing beams for the shorter spans.
7 Shipping prefabricated units and service girders.
8 Storing beams.
9 Manufacture of shuttering for the pier caps.
10 Joinery shops.
11 Workshops.
12 Stores.
13 General storage yard.
14 Control station for floating equipment.
15 Assembling of shuttering, etc., for the cantilever spans.
16 Site office.
17 Laboratories, first aid station, canteen.
18 Camp for workmen and their families.
19 Bridge under construction.

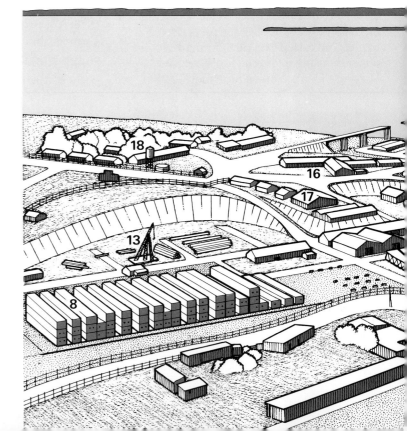

Two views of the Greta Bridge at Keswick, Cumbria, England. Formwork must be built to support concrete spans being cast and reinforced on site.

Concrete structures, of course, contain large quantities of steel. (A typical figure for every 10,000 cubic yards, or 7645 cubic metres, of concrete is 1000 tonnes of steel reinforcements. There will also be 10,000 feet, or 3048 metres, of pre-stressing cable.) But care is taken to make sure that none of the steel is exposed, and also to prevent the development of cracks which might let water seep inside.

The bridge in the pictures on this page was constructed span by span on site. After each span was erected, and the pre-stressing cables were operating, the formwork (see Glossary) was taken down and moved to the next span. However, the sections of the bridge shown on page 12 were made in the factory and then brought to the site, where they were stressed and connected to each other with concrete joints.

Concrete beams were used in the shorter spans of the Lake Maracaibo Bridge, Venezuela, one of the great engineering achievements of the century (see pages 24/25). The bridge has a total of 134 spans.

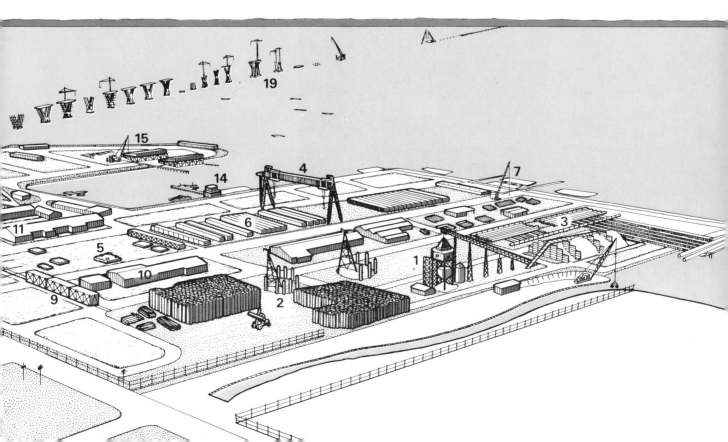

 # Steel arches

The name of Alexandre Gustave Eiffel (died 1923) is popularly associated with his Tower, which still dominates the centre of Paris. But his earlier achievements include a string of viaducts across very difficult, mountainous country in Central France. The region was rich in minerals, and railways were the most suitable form of transport. As always, winds were the great hazard: a bridge several hundred feet high is exposed to wind forces much greater than those found at ground level. To help him understand these problems, Eiffel set up meteorological stations throughout France. Later he was to be one of the first men to construct a wind tunnel.

His most celebrated bridge is the Garabit Viaduct (completed in 1884), 480 feet (146 metres) high in a valley so windswept that trains were not allowed to pass over it at speeds greater than 20 mph (32 kmph). To reduce wind-resistance, Eiffel used an open truss girder that allowed winds to pass through the structure, and he placed the track a little below the top, so that if there was a derailment the train would not fall right off the bridge. The two sides of the arch are deepest at the crown, and slope outwards towards the base, which is three times as wide as the crown. This was done to increase stability. The lower ends of the arch rest upon hinges, to allow for expansion and contraction during changes in temperature.

Eiffel's railway viaduct at Garabit, Central France. The year after this was completed he designed the inner structure for the Statue of Liberty in New York.

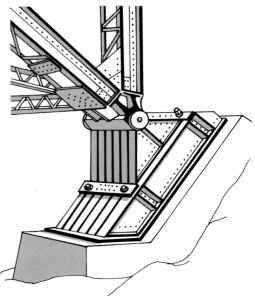

One of the massive hinged bearings of the Zambezi Bridge, Zambia/Zimbabwe, completed in 1907. The hinges allow for the expansion and contraction that occur under changing temperatures.

Left: The Ohmishima Bridge, Japan, has a span of 1014 feet (309 metres). It is the first of several bridges that connect the Japanese main islands of Honshu and Shikoku.

The building of Sydney Harbour Bridge
Two cranes begin to move out towards each other across the Harbour. The growing arch is held in place by steel cables carried down 100 feet (30.5 metres) into the rock.

The cranes lift the steelwork from the water and move their way up the bridge, erecting it ahead of them. Each half-arch weighs 14,000 tonnes. Just before the two halves were to be joined – and were cantilevered 800 feet (244 metres) out from the shore – a gale blew up. But the structure was so sturdy that it suffered no harm.

When the two halves have been joined, the cranes withdraw, fixing the deck and hangers in place as they go.

The completed bridge. To test its strength 72 locomotives were arranged on the tracks in a way which would produce the maximum strain.

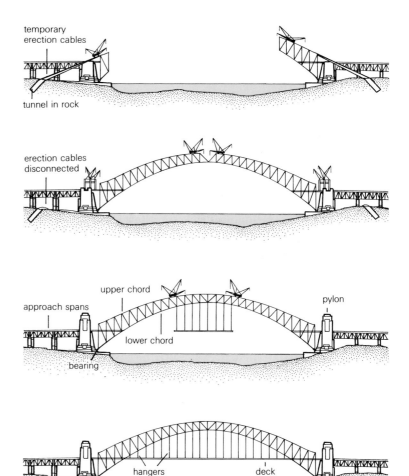

This *two-hinged* design has since been widely adopted, notably in Sydney Harbour Bridge, Australia, which carries an exceptionally heavy load of traffic on two railway tracks and ten road lanes. Extra road lanes have now been substituted for two of the rail tracks. The ribs of the arch, like those at Garabit, were built out in sections by the cantilever method, supported during construction by cables tied back to each side.

All modern bridges contain great quantities of steel, most of it invisible inside concrete. Arches are not as popular as in the great days of the Railway Age. But the steel arches remain as engineering triumphs of their time.

The Glen Canyon Bridge, Arizona, is the world's highest steel arch. Its span of 1028 feet (313 metres) is 700 feet (213 metres) above the river.

Concrete arches

When the first concrete arches were built, designers treated the new material just as a cheap subsitute for stone. Concrete was cast into **voussoirs**, as the individual blocks of an arch are called, and assembled with the use of a traditional scaffolding or **staging** to support the growing arch. Whenever possible, the fact that the bridge was made of concrete was disguised, by making it look like stone.

Robert Maillart in Switzerland and Eugène Freyssinet from his base in France completely changed the way in which concrete was used. They cast directly on to the growing arch, so that when it was completed it was a continuous single structure from end to end.

Maillart's most famous bridges were built across steep Alpine gorges where the staging was extremely difficult to erect. It has been said that they could only have been built in Switzerland, where there are families of craftsmen specializing in this dizzy-making work. Maillart's masterpiece, completed in 1930, is the Salginatobel Bridge, whose arch has a span of 292 feet (89 metres). In the traditional arch bridge the arch is constructed first and the deck then laid on top of it. But here the deck and the arch are parts of the same unit. At the centre, the deck is the upper surface and the arch the lower surface of a long hollow box. As the arch curves outward the lower surface and sides of the box separate from the upper surface, and the space between them is left open except for a few remarkably thin walls.

In France, Freyssinet, the pioneer of pre-stressed concrete, developed a new technique for erecting arches. His design for a bridge across the mouth of the Elorn river at Plougastel in Brittany called for three spans of about 600 feet (183 metres). The **formwork**, sometimes called **centering**, in which the concrete arch is formed, was built upon large barges which were floated out into position. To lift the finished arch off the formwork he invented special jacks which afterwards had their oil drained off and replaced with concrete so that they became part of the permanent structure of the bridge.

Scaffolding supports the growing arches of the Ballochmyle Viaduct, Scotland.

Formwork containing the central arch of Freyssinet's bridge at Plougastel is floated out on two barges. The bridge was completed in 1930.

Maillart's bridge over the Salgina Gorge. Set against their mountain background, Maillart's bridges are both beautiful and amazing.

In 1964 Freyssinet's jacks were used to lift the first concrete arch ever to span 1000 feet (305 metres). This was the Gladesville Bridge at Sydney, within sight of the famous steel arch harbour bridge. Gladesville was also the first concrete arch for many years in which the old voussoir system was used, but the voussoirs in this case were large hollow boxes – the largest being 22 feet (7 metres) long by 20 feet (6 metres) wide by 11 feet (3 metres) high. They were cast and hardened in a nearby factory, then floated out to the site where steel staging had been built across the river, leaving a small channel free for shipping. The voussoirs were hoisted one by one into position and cemented to their neighbours to form the four mighty ribs of the arch. On a good day five or six would be placed in position.

As more has become known about its behaviour under stress, and as methods have been invented to increase its strength, concrete has taken its rightful place as a material calling for its own special forms of bridge with their own unique beauty.

Left: The temporary steel structure used to support the Gladesville Bridge during construction. A navigation channel of 200 feet (61 metres) is spanned by steel trusses.

The completed Gladesville Bridge.

Suspension bridges

Suspension bridges attract attention because they 'bridge the unbridgeable'. Two 19th-century examples are the Clifton Suspension Bridge spanning the Clifton Gorge at Bristol, designed by Isambard Kingdom Brunel when he was only twenty-four; and the Brooklyn Bridge (1883) over the East River in New York, whose 1600-ft (488-metre) span, designed by the father and son team of John Augustus and Washington A. Roebling, astonished the world. Modern achievements include the bridging of three strongly tidal estuaries in Britain – the Forth, the Severn and the Humber; the bridge near the mouth of the fast-flowing Zaire River in Africa; and the 3524-foot (1074-metre) bridge across the Bosporus at Istanbul.

The longer the span the taller are the towers which have to support the cables in the most efficient curve. And to give the cables a secure anchorage the ends must be buried deep in the rock or housed within a massive reinforced concrete structure. One of the anchorage blocks for the Humber Bridge (designed by Freeman Fox & Partners and opened in 1981) is 213 feet (65 metres) long by 118 feet (36 metres) wide and stands on foundations 69 feet (21 metres) below ground level. The blocks for the Matadi Bridge across the Zaire (designed by the Japanese company Ishikawajima-Harima Heavy Industries Limited, and opened in 1983) contain nearly 65,397 cubic yards (50,000 cubic metres) of concrete. Within the anchorage structure the cables pass over the splay saddles and divide into separate strands which are individually fixed to the back wall of the anchorage.

Construction of cable anchorage frames for the Matadi Bridge, Zaire. The frames will later be embedded in concrete. Beyond them the splay saddles have reached a quarter of their final height.

The Bosporus Bridge at Istanbul, Turkey, connects Europe to Asia at the south of the Black Sea. Over 100,000 vehicles cross the bridge each day.

Twin, hollow caissons form the foundations for the south tower of the Humber Bridge. The caissons were sunk 118 feet (36 metres) below the river bed and plugged with concrete slabs.

Wherever possible, bridges are designed so that the piers can be built on dry land. This avoids the many potential difficulties of working in water. When foundations have to be dug below water level a relatively dry working environment may be provided by using **caissons**. These are gigantic steel and concrete cylinders lowered on to the river bed and progressively sunk as the rock is excavated beneath them. Water is kept out by increasing the air pressure within the caisson. In the early days, builders who had been working below ground returned too quickly to normal air pressure and suffered internal injuries – some of them fatal – from caisson disease, the so-called 'bends'.

The Humber Bridge, now the world's longest span, is unusual in having concrete towers. Most other suspension bridges have towers constructed of hollow steel boxes. Sections of the towers are raised into position by special cranes that climb with the tower, building one section then climbing upwards to build the next.

The reinforced concrete towers of the Humber Bridge were built from a platform which climbed up the tower, building the two legs simultaneously. The cross-beams were then added, starting with the top one and working downwards.

A truck crane was used to construct the first six stages of the towers of the Matadi Bridge. Then a hoist was installed to lift the upper cross-beam and a jib crane to a temporary support. The lower cross-beam was next lifted into position. The jib crane built the higher stages (7–10) and was hoisted up until the upper cross-beam could be placed in its permanent position.

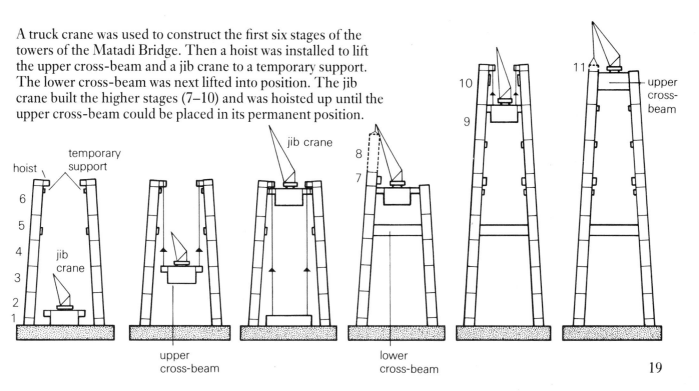

Suspension bridges

After the anchorages have been prepared and the towers erected, the placing of the cables can begin. Each cable contains a number of separate strands made up of a hundred or more steel wires. In the cables of the Matadi Bridge in Zaire there are 54 strands, each of 127 wires, 5mm (⅕″) in diameter. The Humber Bridge cables contain only 37 strands, but each one has 404 wires, making a total for each cable of 14,948 wires.

When steel wire is drawn – that is, stretched – its strength increases, so that a cable made up of close-packed wires will be stronger than a solid rod of the same size. It is this property of steel wire that has made the very long-span suspension bridges possible.

First of all a pilot rope is taken across the river by boat. A hauling rope is pulled across. And finally a catwalk rope is attached to the tops of the towers. Two catwalks are then constructed a few feet beneath the eventual position of the cables.

The air-spinning method of placing cables was perfected more than a century ago by John A. Roebling (see page 18). A continuous loop of rope is hung across the river and two spinning-wheels are attached to it at opposite ends. A section of wire is then pulled off its reel and looped around the spinning-wheel. The free end is then anchored. As the wheel travels across the river it pulls more wire off the reel, so that each wheel lays two thicknesses as it crosses the river. When a reel is exhausted, the end of the first wire is joined to the beginning of the second, so that the cable becomes one continuous wire. The joints, secured by special clamps, are evenly distributed throughout the span.

Two steel-mesh catwalks in position on the Humber Bridge.

John A. Roebling designed the air-spinning method for placing the cables on the Brooklyn Bridge, New York. Here, two spinning wheels take four wires (numbered 1 and 2, 3 and 4) across the river in one go.

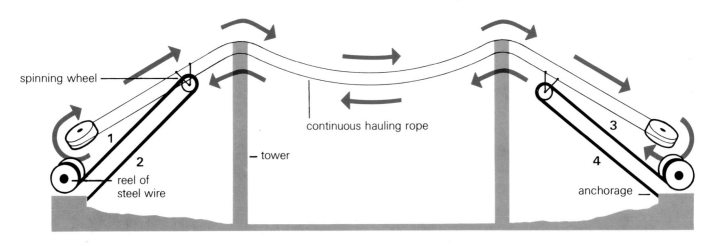

spinning wheel

continuous hauling rope

– tower

reel of steel wire

3

4

anchorage

1

2

Above: Two wires are pulled across the river by the spinning wheel.

Above right: Each wire is laid into place in the saddle at the tower top.

Below: When spinning is completed, the cable is compressed into a circular shape, coated with red lead paste, and wrapped with steel galvanized wire.

Below right: Giant bands are placed round the cables and the hanger ropes are attached.

This process is continued until a strand is completed, and it is started again with the next strand. When all strands are in position they are packed tightly together, covered with wrapping wire, and painted. Cable bands are clamped to them at regular intervals to carry the hanger ropes, or suspenders, that will hold the deck.

For all the very long span bridges – such as the Verrazano, Humber and Severn, the cables have been air-spun. An alternative is bringing the wire to the site already assembled into strands. The strands are then pulled across the river, one at a time. This method has been used for many smaller span bridges, such as the Matadi Bridge in Zaire, and may eventually replace air-spinning altogether because it cuts the time which men have to spend on the catwalks, working in harsh and hazardous conditions. Of course, any shipping in the area has to be kept clear while the strands are lifted.

Suspension bridges

For many years the typical deck for a suspension bridge was a **truss** (see page 7), an arrangement of horizontal and vertical girders stiffened by diagonals. The early example of the Brooklyn Bridge was followed by the great American suspension bridges of the 1920s and 30s. The sheer weight of the steel in these decks was enough to keep the structure rigid, even in strong winds.

To enable longer span bridges to be built, shallower girder decks were introduced in the 1930s and were much admired for their elegance of line. Then came the Tacoma Narrows Bridge – 'Galloping Gertie' – with its deck only 8 feet (2.4 metres) deep on a span of 2800 feet (853 metres). After its sensational collapse in 1940 engineers returned to more conservative designs, and no chances were taken with the second Tacoma Bridge (1950) which was given a truss deck 33 feet (10 metres) deep.

To discover ways of improving truss design, engineers used wind tunnels. As a result, all but one of the great suspension bridges of the 1950s and 60s have been built with deep trusses. The side panels and cross panels are left open, and there are lengthways vents in the deck to allow wind to pass through. The exception is the Severn Bridge (1966), which introduced a new type of deck structure, the aerodynamic box-girder.

Deck sections for the Humber Bridge under construction. Each box section was assembled next to its eventual neighbour to give an accurate fit when erected.

Above: The Matadi Bridge was designed to carry rail traffic within the truss and a road above it. Here the lifting beam manoeuvres part of the deck into position.

Right: Lifting a box section on the Humber Bridge. The upper surface of the box will become a 4-lane carriageway; the panels cantilevered out from each side form the footways and cycle tracks.

The deck steadily takes shape, as work is carried out simultaneously in the side spans, from anchorages, and from the the middle of the centre span, towards the towers.

A truss is designed to let air pass harmlessly *through* the structure. Because of its shape, the box-girder allows air to pass harmlessly *around* it. Box-girders use less steel, thus reducing weight as well as cost; repainting and other maintenance is easier; so is the work of construction, because large sections are assembled in the factory.

The bridge across the Lillebaelt in Denmark (1970) has a box-girder deck. So has the first Bosporus Bridge (1973) and the Humber Bridge (1981). The second Bosporus Bridge, for which the design is already underway, will also have a development of the box-girder deck. If a bridge is ever built across the English Channel it is likely to follow the same style.

However, when a suspension bridge is to carry rail traffic, the truss deck is still preferred, with the railway generally inside the truss and the road above it. As with box-girders, manufacturers of truss systems are also now introducing pre-formed sections. Indeed, pre-assembly, with its valuable saving in time and labour, is the future trend in all areas of bridge-building.

Adjacent box sections are welded together, mostly from the inside.

From the Control Room the operator can see the approach roads and the toll booths. Close at hand are television cameras and monitoring systems.

Cantilever bridges

Cantilever bridges have existed for over two thousand years in China and Tibet but they were built of timber, and not designed for heavy loads. The problem of how to build long spans rigid enough to carry rail traffic was not solved until cheap, reliable steel was introduced in the 1870s.

Benjamin Baker, the principal designer of the Forth Rail Bridge in Scotland (completed in 1890), was an early enthusiast for cantilever bridges. At lectures he would demonstrate how a cantilever works by using two colleagues and himself as the piers and the suspended span.

Benjamin Baker demonstrating the system of counterbalances in a cantilever.

The Oosterschelde Bridge joins the islands of the Schelde delta to the mainland of Holland. The cantilever element is not always obvious in modern bridges.

The first modern cantilever bridge was built at Hassfurt in Germany, followed a few years later by a railway cantilever across the Niagara river in Canada. But the bridge across the estuary of the river Forth dwarfed its predecessors – and its two spans of 1710 feet (521 metres) held the length record for nearly thirty years. Not only is the bridge strong in effect, it *looks* strong. Some of its tubes of steel are 12 feet (4 metres) in diameter. As in the viaducts designed by Eiffel (see page 14), its legs are set far apart and its towers slope in towards the top. The cantilevers were built out symmetrically from the towers, to keep the forces balanced. When the two halves of the central suspended span were in contact they were riveted together. The cost of maintenance for such a gigantic structure is enormous. No sooner has it been repainted, than it is time to start all over again.

The five cable-supported cantilever spans of the Maracaibo Bridge are flanked by shorter cantilever spans resting on H-type trestle piers. As the legs of the piers shorten they pass into the V-type. The construction site shown on pages 12 and 13 lies to the right. To the left stand a further 75 spans resting on plain piers.

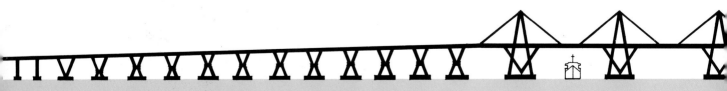

Since the Forth Bridge, several cantilevers have been built of steel, but more recently pre-stressed concrete has been used. The Oosterschelde Bridge in Holland (see page 24) is a three-mile (5-km) pre-stressed concrete structure consisting of 48 spans. All the spans are identical, which means that the units could be mass-produced, thus cutting down on costs.

Some cantilever bridges are deceptive in appearance. On the Lake Maracaibo Bridge in Venezuela there are cable stays, but it is still of cantilever type. The spans of this great bridge – which stretches for 5 miles (8 kms) across the mouth of Lake Maracaibo – increase in stages from 120 feet (37 metres) to the five central spans of 780 feet (238 metres). Cables tied to the tops of the central towers provide additional support for the cantilevered decks, allowing them to be long without being deep. The concrete was prepared in a floating mixing plant, then carried up the bridge, and poured into forms supported on a steel service girder. In order to keep the balance right, a precise sequence of concreting had to be followed.

Approach spans of the Maracaibo Bridge consist of shorter cantilever beams connected by a 150-foot (45-metre) 'fish-belly' beam. Connecting beams of the same length were used in the main span, and elsewhere on the bridge. To reduce costs, the design used standardized units wherever possible.

The five main cantilever spans of the Maracaibo Bridge rest upon X-type trestle piers. They are also supported by cables tied to the top of the A-frame towers. Nowhere else are the towers connected with the cantilever span or with the X-frames. The height of the roadway gives a navigation clearance of 150 feet (45 metres).

Stage by stage

The various stages in building a bridge are planned so that there are no unnecessary periods of inactivity, or hold-ups. This can be seen by following the 'timetable' of a bridge's construction. We have chosen the Matadi Bridge in Zaire. Its span of 1706 feet (520 metres) makes it the largest suspension bridge in Africa, and materials had to be brought 10,000 miles (16,093 kms) by sea from Japan.

1971–1976   The firm of Ishikawajima-Harima Heavy Industries works out a scheme for building a bridge at Matadi. This includes costing and arranging the necessary finance. The site is surveyed. The first design is made. A model is built and tested in a wind tunnel. Materials are tested.

November 1978   The Republic of Zaire appoints the Japanese consortium of IHI Limited, Mitsubishi, and Kawasaki, to build the bridge.

February 1979   Building of the construction base, workers' houses and amenities begins.

November 1979   Excavation for anchorages and piers begins. The building of access roads begins.

December 1979   In Japan, the manufacture of anchorages and towers begins.

June 1980   Excavation for the piers is completed.

July 1980   The first ship arrives at Matadi Port with cable anchor frames and tower anchor frames.

September 1980   In Japan the manufacture of cable wire begins.

October 1980   Concrete work for the base of the towers is completed. The second ship arrives with tower panels and reinforcement for anchorages.

November 1980   Excavation for the anchorages is completed. Construction of the towers begins. In Japan, manufacture of the deck girders begins.

February 1981   The first-stage concreting for the anchorages is completed.

March 1981   The cable anchor frames are installed. The second stage of concreting begins.

April 1981   The towers are completed.

July 1981   The third ship arrives with tower top saddles, splay saddles and cable. The pilot rope is taken across the river.

August 1981   The construction of catwalks for installing cables begins.

September 1981   The catwalks are completed.

October 1981   The pulling out of the cable strands begins. (54 strands to each cable, each containing 127 prefabricated parallel wires.)

November 1981   The concrete work for the anchorages is completed, except for the final slab-work. The fourth ship arrives, with deck girders for side spans.

January 1982   The pulling of the cable strands is completed.

March 1982   The fifth ship arrives with half the deck girders for the main span.

May 1982   The side spans – cable bands, hanger ropes and deck girders – are completed.

June 1982   The erection of deck girders for the central span begins, proceeding from the towers towards the centre. The paintwork begins.

July 1982   The sixth ship arrives with the remainder of the girders for the main span.

September 1982   The deck girders for the central span are completed. The picture shows a deck girder being brought into alignment on the centre span.

November 1982   The cable wrapping is completed.

December 1982   Dismantling of the tower top cranes and scaffolding begins. The access roads are completed.

February 1983   The asphalting of the deck is completed.

March 1983   The fitting of the concrete kerbs, the hand railings, and the lighting work, are completed. The paintwork is completed. The loading test on the roadway is carried out.

April 1983   The tightening of the cable bands is completed. The erection equipment is dismantled; temporary facilities are removed. Equipment is packed for return to Japan. The site is cleared.

May 1983   The ceremonial opening of the bridge.

Who builds bridges?

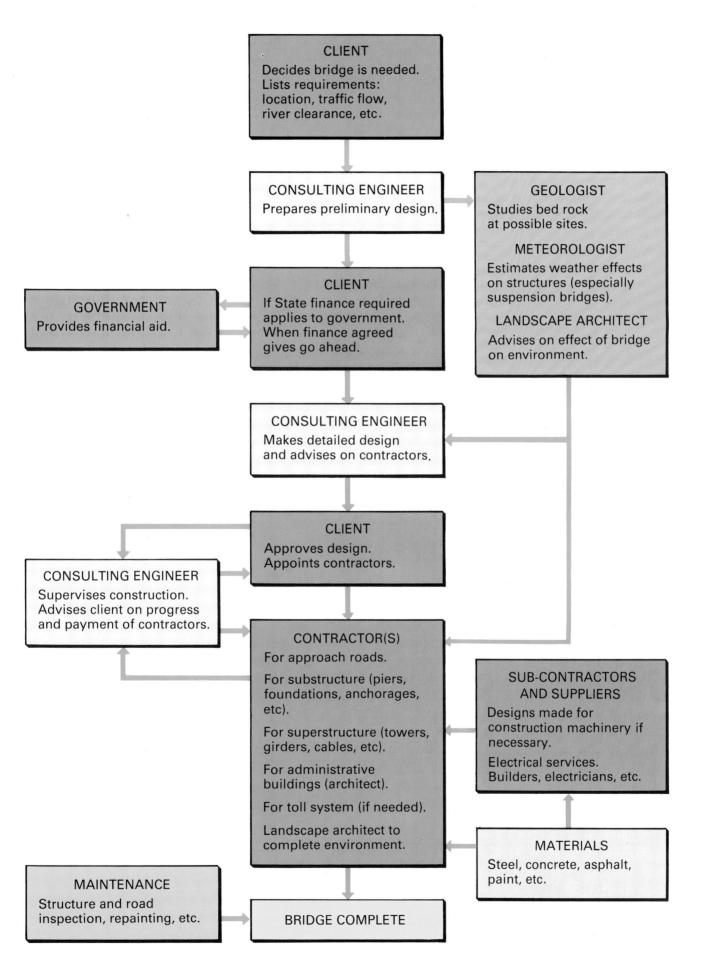

CLIENT
Decides bridge is needed. Lists requirements: location, traffic flow, river clearance, etc.

CONSULTING ENGINEER
Prepares preliminary design.

GEOLOGIST
Studies bed rock at possible sites.

METEOROLOGIST
Estimates weather effects on structures (especially suspension bridges).

LANDSCAPE ARCHITECT
Advises on effect of bridge on environment.

CLIENT
If State finance required applies to government. When finance agreed gives go ahead.

GOVERNMENT
Provides financial aid.

CONSULTING ENGINEER
Makes detailed design and advises on contractors.

CLIENT
Approves design. Appoints contractors.

CONSULTING ENGINEER
Supervises construction. Advises client on progress and payment of contractors.

CONTRACTOR(S)
For approach roads.

For substructure (piers, foundations, anchorages, etc).

For superstructure (towers, girders, cables, etc).

For administrative buildings (architect).

For toll system (if needed).

Landscape architect to complete environment.

SUB-CONTRACTORS AND SUPPLIERS
Designs made for construction machinery if necessary.

Electrical services. Builders, electricians, etc.

MATERIALS
Steel, concrete, asphalt, paint, etc.

MAINTENANCE
Structure and road inspection, repainting, etc.

BRIDGE COMPLETE

Great bridges of the world

Australia

Sydney Harbour Bridge. 1932. One of the world's most famous landmarks. Steel through-arch, which took eight years to build.
Gladesville Bridge, Sydney. 1964. The world's longest concrete arch, with a 1000-ft (305-metre) span.

Belgium
Ourthe Bridge, Liège. Among the first bridges to be built of reinforced concrete, for the 1905 Exhibition.

Canada
Quebec (Railway) Bridge. After two disastrous failures, an 1800-ft (549-metre) cantilever was finally built here in 1918 and became the world's longest span.
Lions Gate Bridge, Vancouver. 1939. 2778-ft (847-metre) span suspension bridge using cables made of wire ropes instead of parallel wires.

Denmark
Storstrøm Bridge. 1937. Fifty spans over two miles (3.2 kms) connecting Copenhagen with the mainland of Denmark.
Lillebaelt Bridge. 1970. The second major bridge to use an aerodynamically shaped box-girder deck.

France
Pont du Gard, Nîmes. The best-known surviving Roman aqueduct. Three tiers of arches 900-feet (274-metres) long.
Pont St. Bénézet. The 'Pont d'Avignon' celebrated in a popular song. Built in 1177. Four of the original 20 arches and a chapel still remain.

Pont Valentré, Cahors. Mediaeval war-bridge, flanked with battlements and towers.

Paris. Of its many elegant bridges, old and new, the **Pont Neuf** (the 'New' Bridge) is the oldest.
Limoges and elsewhere in central France: several railway viaducts and many bridges designed by Gustave Eiffel.
Plougastel, Brittany. Three arches, each of 567-feet (173-metres) across the River Elorn. 1930. One of the many fine concrete bridges designed by Eugène Freyssinet.
Marne Bridges. Long, single-span 'portal frame' bridges in pre-stressed concrete were built by Freyssinet in the 1940s at Luzancy, Esbly, Annet, Tribardou, Changis and Ussey.

West Germany
Cologne, Bonn, etc. Cable-stayed bridges of various types built across the Rhine.

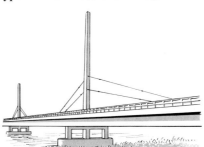

Norderelbe Bridge, Hamburg. 1962. The first cable-stayed bridge to have its cables built in a single, central line.

Holland
Oosterschelde Bridge. 1965. A causeway connecting Flushing with Rotterdam. Three miles (4.8 kms) long, with forty-eight identical 312-foot (95-metre) spans in pre-stressed concrete.

India

Howrah Bridge, Calcutta. 1943. Cantilever span of 1500 feet (457 metres) across the Hooghly River.

Italy
Rome. Several bridges stand on ancient Roman foundations. The **Ponte dei Quattro Capi** leading to Tiber Island is the former Pons Fabricius (62 BC).

Ponte di Augusto, Rimini. The best-preserved Roman bridge in Italy, built at the time of the Emperor Augustus.
Ponte Vecchio, Florence. 'The Old Bridge', built about 1340, lined with jewellers' and goldsmiths' shops.
Ponte Santa Trinità, Florence. Built in 1567 with three remarkably shallow arches, destroyed in World War II but restored to its original design.
Rialto Bridge, Venice. Built in 1588. Famous stepped bridge across the Grand Canal.
Bridge of Sighs, Venice. Built in 1597 to connect the Doge's Palace with the Prisons.
In the 1960s and '70s many beautiful and spectacular autostrada (motorway) bridges were built in Italy.

Portugal
Douro Bridge, Oporto. 1963. Concrete bridge with a span of 891 feet (271 metres). When built it was the longest concrete arch span in the world.

Ponte 25 de Abril (Tagus Bridge) Lisbon. Suspension bridge with a 3323-foot (1013-metre) centre span carrying rail as well as road traffic. One of its piers had to be sunk 240 feet (73 metres) below the river level.

Spain

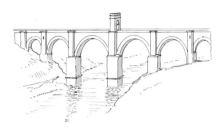

Alcantara. 6-arch Roman bridge across the Tagus. The name comes from Al Kantarah, Moorish for 'the Bridge'.
Segovia. Two tiers of this ancient aqueduct are still in good repair.

Sweden
Sandö Bridge. 1943. Attractive concrete bridge over the Angerman River bordering Norway. For twenty years the 866-foot (264-metre) concrete arch was the world's longest.
Strömsund Bridge. 1956. The world's first cable-stayed bridge, with a span of 600 feet (183 metres).

Switzerland

Bridges by Robert Maillart, pioneer designer of concrete bridges, can be seen in Zurich, Schwandbach, Salginatobel.

Turkey
Bosporus Bridge, Istanbul. 1974. A suspension bridge of 3524 feet (1074 metres) connecting Europe and Asia. It now carries 115,000 vehicles each day. Design for a second bridge has already begun (1984).

United Kingdom
Iron Bridge, Coalbrookdale. 1779. The world's first iron bridge.
Menai Suspension Bridge, North Wales. 1826. Designed by Thomas Telford, builder of hundreds of road bridges and known as 'the father of civil engineering'.
Conway Tubular Bridge, North Wales. 1848. Robert Stephenson's trial run for the Britannia Bridge further along the coast.
Britannia Tubular Bridge, North Wales. 1850. Pioneering design by Stephenson across the Menai Straits. Still carrying rail traffic through its iron tubes.
Chepstow, South Wales. 1952. Iron truss rail bridge across the River Wye, designed by Isambard Kingdom Brunel.

Clifton Suspension Bridge, Bristol. 1859. Suspension bridge designed by Brunel and constructed after his death.
Forth Rail Bridge, Scotland. 1890. Colossal steel cantilever bridge. Its two spans of 1710 feet (521 metres) each were the longest in the world for nearly thirty years.

London Bridge. Rebuilt many times. The famous many-arched bridge, where traitors' heads used to be exhibited on poles, was begun in 1176. It was finally replaced by a 5-arched bridge in 1831; this was later sold to the USA and now stands across Lake Havasu in Arizona. The present London Bridge was opened in 1973.

Albert Bridge, London. 1873. An early example of a bridge which uses cable stays as well as suspension cables.

Tower Bridge, London. 1894. Restored and reopened in 1982. A popular tourist attraction. The machinery for raising its drawbridges (bascules) is housed in the piers below the mediaeval-style towers.
Waterloo Bridge, London. 1942. Its graceful five spans look like arches, but the outer four are actually girder beams and the central span is simply supported on two cantilever arms.
Forth Road Bridge, Scotland. 1964. Britain's largest truss-deck suspension bridge.
Severn Bridge. 1966. Linking England and Wales with a span of 3240 feet (988 metres). The first suspension bridge to use the streamlined box-girder deck.
Usk Bridge, Newport, South Wales. First true cable-stayed bridge in Britain, with a span of 500 feet (152 metres).
Humber Bridge. 1981. With its 4625-foot (1410-metre) span it is the world's longest-span bridge.

United States
St Louis Bridge. 1874. Captain James Eads' great bridge across the Mississippi. The first to make full use of steel. Still in use.

Brooklyn Bridge, New York. 1883. Suspension bridge across the East River designed by J. A. and W. Roebling. It has a span of 1600 feet (488 metres).

Hell Gate Bridge, New York.
1916. Steel through-arch carrying four rail tracks across the East River, designed by Gustave Lindenthal and for many years the longest arch span (577 feet or 176 metres) in the world.
George Washington Bridge, New York. 1931. Designed by O. H. Ammann, with a 3500-foot (1067-metre) span across the Hudson River. It pioneered modern cable-spinning techniques.
Bayonne Bridge, New York. Connecting New York (State) and Staten Island. It is 2 feet, or 0.6 metres, longer (by intention) than the Sydney Harbour Bridge.
Verrazano Narrows Bridge, New York. 1964. Suspension Bridge across the entrance to New York Harbour with a span of 4260 feet (1298 metres). Designed by O. H. Ammann. It superseded the Golden Gate as the world's longest bridge.

Bay Bridge, San Francisco. 1936. A 4½-mile (7.2 km) structure containing two suspension bridges, each of 2310 feet (704 metres) and a cantilever bridge of 1400 feet (427 metres).
Golden Gate Bridge, San Francisco. 1937. Another of the world's most famous landmarks, which for nearly thirty years was the longest span (4200 feet or 1280 metres) in the world.
Chesapeake Bay, Maryland. 1964. Seventeen miles (27 kms) of tunnel and bridge built of pre-stressed concrete.
Luling Bridge, New Orleans. A span of 2746 feet (837 metres)

across the Mississippi. The longest cable-stayed bridge in America.

Venezuela
Maracaibo Lake Bridge. 1962. Five miles (8 kms) of bridges with five cantilever spans of 710 feet (216 metres) each at the centre. A major work achieved in reinforced concrete.

Zaire
Matadi Bridge. 1983. 2369 feet (722 metres). The longest suspension bridge in Africa.

Zambia/Zimbabwe

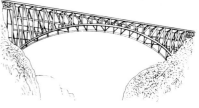

Zambezi Bridge. 1907. 500-foot (152-metre) steel arch.

The world's longest bridges

	feet	metres	
			Suspension bridges
1981	4625	1410	Humber, England
1964	4260	1298	Verrazano Narrows, USA
1937	4200	1280	Golden Gate, USA
			Cantilever bridges
1917	1800	549	Quebec, Canada
1890	1710	521	Firth of Forth (railway), Scotland
1974	1644	501	Commodore John Barry, Delaware, USA
			Steel arch bridges
1981	1700	518	New River Gorge, West Virginia, USA
1931	1675	511	Bayonne, New Jersey, USA
1932	1670	509	Sydney Harbour, Australia
			Continuous steel box-girder bridges
1974	984	300	Ponte Presidente Costa da Silva, Rio de Janeiro, Brazil
1956	837	255	Sava, Yugoslavia
1966	831	253	Zoo, Cologne, Germany
			Cable-stayed bridges
1985	1500	457	Yokahama Bay, Japan
1986/7	1500	457	Hooghly, Calcutta, India
1984	1440	439	Vancouver, Canada
			Concrete arch bridges
1979	1280	390	KRK Zagreb, Yugoslavia
1964	1000	305	Gladesville, Sydney
1964	951	290	Foz-do-Iguaçu, Amizade, Brazil

Glossary

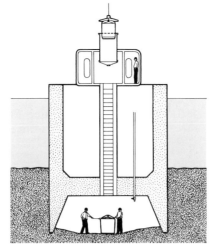

Abutment The structure where an arch reaches the ground and meets the resistance that keeps it stable. Generally, the structure at the ends of any bridge.

Air-spinning A method used in the making of cables for a suspension bridge. The strands of wire are passed back and forth across the span, until the cable is built up to the diameter, and strength that is required.

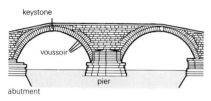

Arch A curved structure of which the weight at its centre is carried outwards to the ground.

Aqueduct A bridge, or line of bridges, carrying a channel of water across a valley.

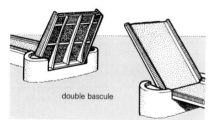

double bascule

Bascule A form of drawbridge with a counterbalance at the end which is hinged. When the counterbalance is allowed to sink, the free end rises.

Beam A straight structure supporting a deck or roadway. In cross-section it can have various shapes – for example, T-beam, I-beam, etc. It is often made up of a number of smaller beams. Also known as a **girder**. It is termed a 'simply-supported' beam when it rests on a pier at each end and a 'continuously supported' beam when it rests on many piers.

Box-girder A hollow girder, or beam, lighter than a solid one, making more efficient use of the material.

Caisson A structure for keeping out water while deep foundations

for a bridge are dug. In the lower working chamber water is kept out by increasing the air pressure.

Cantilever A beam that is free at one end and counterbalanced at the other.

Cast iron An alloy of iron with up to 3% carbon, which is cast or poured into moulds. Excellent in **compression** but unreliable in tension.

Coffer dam A structure for keeping out water to allow excavation in ground which is normally submerged. It differs from a caisson in that it is open to the air and is therefore unsuitable for deep working.

Compression A force which tends to reduce or shorten something by pressure. The upper surface of a simply-supported girder is 'under compression' because the weight tends to bend the middle of the girder downwards. The underside of an arch is 'under compression'. (The opposite to compression is **tension**.)

Creep The gradual alteration in shape of certain materials, especially concrete, while under pressure.

Deck Generally the top side of a **girder** which provides the running surface for vehicles.

Formwork The structure built to form, or shape, concrete on a bridge and to hold it while it hardens.

Hangers (Also known as Suspenders.) The wires or bars by means of which the deck is hung from the cables in a suspension bridge.

Pier A support for the middle spans of a beam bridge or arch bridge. The word is also used for the base or foundation of the tower of a suspension bridge or a cantilever bridge.

Pre-stressed concrete A development from reinforced concrete. Steel wires within the wet concrete are stretched and held fast until the concrete hardens. The concrete then keeps the wires in a state of **tension**, and the wires keep the concrete in a state of **compression**. Alternatively, the steel cables are threaded through tubes in the hardened concrete, and after being tensioned are grouted into place for protection.

Reinforced concrete Concrete which contains steel rods, bars, wires or mesh to provide tensile strength.

Shrinkage The shortening of concrete which occurs while it dries and hardens.

Swing bridge A method of bridging a waterway when high approach roads are impractical.

Tension A force which tends to lengthen something. The lower surface of a simply-supported beam is 'under tension', and so are the cables and hangers of a suspension bridge. (The opposite to tension is **compression**.)

Truss An arrangement of short beams or girders which give strength to one another and which together make up a long beam.

Viaduct A bridge, or line of bridges, carrying a road or railway.

Voussoirs The individual stones or concrete sections which form the curve of an arch.

Wrought iron 'Wrought' means 'worked'. Iron which has been hammered into shape has great strength under **tension**. It was used for the hangers and cables of early suspension bridges.

Index

Acknowledgements

Illustration credits
Photographs: J Allan Cash Photolibrary 24 (centre); Bilfinger & Berger International Division 25; Cement & Concrete Association 17 (top); Construction News Magazine 12 (top); Daily Telegraph Colour Library/Len Rhodes 3 (top); England Scene Colour Picture Library 2 (top); Freeman Fox & Partners 10, 11 (top); Handford Photography 9 (top); Robert Harding Picture Library/ Walter Rawlings 15, 18 (bottom); IHI Company Limited 5 (bottom), 14 (bottom left), 18 (top), 22 (bottom left), 26; International Maunsell Group of Consulting Engineers 17; A F Kersting 14 (top); David Lee Photography Limited 19, 20, 21, 22 (top), 22 (bottom right), 23; Arthur Lockwood 16 (top), 24 (top); Science Museum 11 (bottom); Ronald Sheridan Photo-Library 2 (bottom); The Visual Link 13; Derek Widdicombe Countrywide Photographic Library 6 (top).
Diagrams and drawings: Ray Burrows 4, 5, 10, 12, 13, 15, 19, 20, 24, 25, 31; Gillian Newing 7, 8 (bottom), 9 (bottom) from 'The Book of Bridges' Marshall Cavendish 1976, 14, 17 (bottom right), 27; Carole Vincer 8 (top), 28, 29, 30.

How Bridges Are Made
© Threshold Books Limited, 1985. Reprinted 1989
First published in the United States of America by Facts On File, Inc.,
460 Park Avenue South, New York, NY 10016.
First published in Great Britain by Faber and Faber Limited.

General Editor: Barbara Cooper
The How It Is Made series was conceived, designed and produced by Threshold Books Limited, 661 Fulham Road, London SW6.

Library of Congress Cataloging in Publication Data
Kingston, Jeremy.
    How bridges are made.

    Summary: Illustrates how the five main types of bridges are designed and built and describes the materials and skills used in their construction.
    1. Bridge construction——Juvenile literature.
[1. Bridge construction] I. Title.
TG148.K56   1985   624'.2   84-21054
ISBN 0-8160-0040-9

Typeset by Phoenix Photosetting, Chatham, Kent, England
Printed and bound in Belgium by Henri Proost & Cie PVBA